Lerner SPORTS™

SPORTS VIPs

MEET DEVIN BOOKER

LESLIE HOLLERAN

Lerner Publications ◆ Minneapolis

Lerner Publications Company
An imprint of Lerner Publishing Group, Inc.
241 First Avenue North
Minneapolis, MN 55401 USA

For reading levels and more information, look up this title at www.lernerbooks.com.

Main body text set in Aptifer Slab LT Pro. Typeface provided by Linotype AG.

Editor: Matt Doeden

Library of Congress Cataloging-in-Publication Data

Names: Holleran, Leslie, author.
Title: Meet Devin Booker : Phoenix Suns superstar / Leslie Holleran.
Description: Minneapolis, MN : Lerner Publications, [2023] | Series: Sports VIPs (Lerner Sports) | Includes bibliographical references and index. | Audience: Ages 7–11 years | Audience: Grades 4–6 | Summary: "After leading the Phoenix Suns to the 2021 NBA Finals, guard Devin Booker signed a contract with the team that will pay him more than 200 million dollars by 2028. Explore his life and career"— Provided by publisher.
Identifiers: LCCN 2022054173 (print) | LCCN 2022054174 (ebook) | ISBN 9781728490977 (library binding) | ISBN 9798765604007 (paperback) | ISBN 9798765601433 (ebook)
Subjects: LCSH: Booker, Devin, 1996-—Juvenile literature. | African American basketball players—United States—Biography—Juvenile literature. | Basketball players—United States—Biography—Juvenile literature. | Phoenix Suns (Basketball team)—History—Juvenile literature. | BISAC: JUVENILE NONFICTION / Biography & Autobiography / Sports & Recreation
Classification: LCC GV884.B65 H65 2023 (print) | LCC GV884.B65 (ebook) | DDC 796.323092 [B]—dc23/eng/20230112

LC record available at https://lccn.loc.gov/2022054173
LC ebook record available at https://lccn.loc.gov/2022054174

Manufactured in the United States of America
1-53028-51046-2/28/2023

TABLE OF CONTENTS

CLUTCH SHOT 4

FAST FACTS 5

CHAPTER 1
EARLY LOVE 8

CHAPTER 2
JOINING THE WILDCATS 12

CHAPTER 3
LUCKY 13 16

CHAPTER 4
SHINING BRIGHT 22

DEVIN BOOKER CAREER STATS 28
GLOSSARY 29
SOURCE NOTES 30
LEARN MORE 31
INDEX 32

CLUTCH SHOT

Devin Booker was in peak form. The Phoenix Suns star guard was making shots from all over the court against the Los Angeles Clippers. The two teams were battling for a playoff spot in August 2020 after COVID-19 had forced the National Basketball Association (NBA) to close in March.

The Suns and Clippers were in a close contest through the game's final minutes. With 36 seconds left, the game was tied, 113–113. Booker put the Suns ahead by two points. Then the Clippers tied the score again. It came down to the final possession.

FAST FACTS

DATE OF BIRTH: October 30, 1996

POSITION: shooting guard

LEAGUE: National Basketball Association (NBA)

PROFESSIONAL HIGHLIGHTS: named to the 2016 NBA All-Rookie First Team; won the NBA three-point contest in 2018; the sixth player in NBA history to score 70 or more points in a game

PERSONAL HIGHLIGHTS: attended the University of Kentucky from 2014–2015; was a global ambassador at the 2020 Special Olympics; started his own charity called the Starting Five

Booker drives against Clippers defender Paul George during their game on August 4, 2020.

With six seconds left and the defense closing in, Booker made a difficult fadeaway shot. He landed flat on his back. Then he watched the ball drop into the basket as the buzzer went off. Game over! Booker's teammates rushed to the court to celebrate the game-winning shot. The 117–115 win kept the Suns' playoff hopes alive.

The Suns fell short of the playoffs in 2020. But Booker's strong play had shown that he was a rising star in the league. Bigger and better things lay ahead in Phoenix's future.

Booker shoots the game-winning basket in the Suns' 117–115 victory over the Clippers.

CHAPTER 1

EARLY LOVE

Devin Armani Booker was born on October 30, 1996, in Grand Rapids, Michigan. His parents are Melvin Booker and Veronica Gutierrez. His father was an outstanding

Devin grew up loving basketball. He lived most of the year with his mother in Michigan. He spent summers with his dad in Mississippi. His dad taught him the right way to shoot. Melvin Booker said, "I would never let him shoot any other way but the correct way." Devin practiced and became a good shooter. He was also very competitive and driven to win.

Melvin Booker brings the ball up the court in this 1994 University of Missouri game.

In his first year, Devin joined the Grandville High School varsity basketball team. But he only played one season there. Melvin Booker had become an assistant coach at Moss Point High School in Mississippi. He wanted Devin to live with him and join the team. After his first season, Devin agreed. He moved 1,000 miles (1,600 km) away to live with his dad. There he grew as a player from the knowledge his dad shared with him every day.

SUPER SPORTS SCOOP

Devin Booker was Moss Point High School's all-time leading scorer with 2,518 points. He averaged 30.9 points per game during his senior season.

Booker competes in the three-point contest at the McDonald's All-American Games in 2014.

Booker put his shooting skills to good use. He had a 54-point game his sophomore year. As a junior, he averaged almost 30 points per game. During his senior year, he led Moss Point to an undefeated season and a regional tournament championship. Another highlight was earning McDonald's All-American honors as one of the top high school players in the United States. Devin called it a dream come true.

CHAPTER 2

JOINING THE WILDCATS

By his senior season, Devin stood at 6 feet 5 (2 m). His size and skill made him one of the nation's top high school players. He had scholarship offers from many major universities. He narrowed his top picks to five before his senior year. They were Florida, Kentucky, Michigan, Michigan State, and Missouri.

Kentucky coach John Calipari visited Devin at home in Moss Point to deliver a scholarship offer personally. He also wanted to share what it's like to play for the Wildcats.

"[Calipari] just said that a lot of pressure comes with playing at Kentucky," Devin said. "He said that Big Blue Nation are obviously wild, and if you have a bad game, they're going to get on you. But that's the kind of pressure I like."

Booker (*center*) celebrates with teammate Willie Cauley-Stein (*left*) and coach John Calipari (*right*) after their win over Notre Dame in the 2015 Elite Eight.

Booker goes up for a shot in a 2014 game against North Carolina.

Devin chose Kentucky. He joined his friend Tyler Ulis and two other high school stars, including Karl-Anthony Towns. The players were some of the highest-rated recruits in the US.

In the 2014–2015 season, Booker came off the bench for Kentucky. He played in every game and made a big impact with his great shooting. He sank 58 shots from long range during the season. Five of his three-pointers came in a decisive 83–44 victory over UCLA.

Booker also took his studies seriously. He made the Southeastern Conference (SEC) academic honor roll. He was performing well on and off the court.

The Wildcats didn't disappoint. The team had a 34-0 record in the 2014–2015 regular season. They went on to the National Collegiate Athletic Association (NCAA) tournament. The Wildcats advanced to the Final Four before losing to Wisconsin, 71–64.

Booker's first college basketball season was over. But his career was about to go to a whole new level. It was time to go pro.

SUPER SPORTS SCOOP

Booker was named SEC Sixth Man of the Year in the 2014–2015 season. He was also SEC Freshman of the Week four weeks in a row between January 12 and February 2, 2015.

CHAPTER 3

LUCKY 13

Booker's dream was to play in the NBA. So, after one year at Kentucky, he entered the NBA Draft. Despite not starting any games in college, he was a big prospect. He attended the draft in Brooklyn, New York. His mom, dad, and Coach Calipari were with him. The Phoenix Suns selected him with the 13th pick. Booker was all smiles as he put on an orange Suns hat. He was headed to the NBA.

Booker had an exciting first NBA season. In March, he led all rookies in points and assists. After the season, he made the All-Rookie First Team. He was the first Suns player to be named to the team in more than 10 years.

NBA Commissioner Adam Silver congratulates Booker after the Suns selected him in the 2015 NBA Draft.

His play got even better during his second season. He was making NBA history. He became the youngest player to score 20 points or more in 16 games in a row. In one of those games, Booker scored 27 points in less than eight minutes. He was in the zone.

Booker was turning heads. His coach, Earl Watson, even said that Booker reminded him of NBA legend Kobe Bryant. It was big praise. Bryant was also the player Booker admired most.

SUPER SPORTS SCOOP

On March 24, 2017, the Suns played the Boston Celtics. Booker scored 70 points in the game. He became the sixth and youngest player in NBA history to score 70 points or more in a single game.

Booker dribbles the ball during his rookie season in the NBA. He went on to make the NBA's All-Rookie First Team.

Bryant became a mentor to Booker. "Kobe told me there are no steps skipped in achieving greatness at the highest level," Booker said. "In terms of dieting and working out, it's just about sacrifice. You have to sacrifice things you want." Booker followed that advice. He no longer ate his favorite fast food except as a rare treat.

Booker continued to set personal and NBA records during his third NBA season. He also suffered injuries that kept him off the court at times. In 2018, Booker won the NBA's three-point contest. He set a contest record with 28 points.

Booker plays defense against the Sacramento Kings in a 2015 game.

Booker takes a shot in the 2018 three-point contest. He set a record with 28 points and won the contest.

That season Booker told his team that their days of missing the playoffs were over. The Suns signed Booker on a $158 million contract. He agreed to play for Phoenix for five more years. He wanted to win a title with the team. Suns fans were thrilled to have him.

CHAPTER 4

SHINING BRIGHT

After their strong showing in 2019–2020, the Suns went all in the next season. They traded for star guard Chris Paul. Paul and Booker combined for a strong backcourt.

Booker and the Suns earned a playoff spot and advanced to the Western Conference Finals. They faced the Los Angeles Clippers. Booker was on fire in the first game of the series. The teams were tied going into the fourth quarter. Booker sank a three-pointer early in the quarter and just kept going. He finished the game with 40 points, 13 rebounds, and 11 assists for his first career triple-double. More important, he carried the Suns to a 120–114 victory.

Booker and Chris Paul (*number 3*) teamed up to form a potent backcourt for the Suns.

The Suns went on to win the series, 4–2. Booker scored 22 points in the 130–103 victory that sent the Suns to the NBA Finals. They faced the Milwaukee Bucks for a shot at an NBA title.

Booker shined again in the Finals. In Game 4, he scored 42 points to tie the series at two games each. But the Bucks were too strong for the Suns. They won the next two games to claim the championship. Booker and the Suns had come up short.

SUPER SPORTS SCOOP

Booker played for Team USA at the 2021 Olympic Games in Tokyo, Japan. Team USA brought home a gold medal after beating France, 87–82.

Booker slams one home during a 2022 game against the Boston Celtics.

Phoenix was strong again in 2022. They made it to the Western Conference Semifinals. But they lost to the Dallas Mavericks in a back-and-forth series. Booker had not met his goal of winning the NBA title. But the Suns remained one of the NBA's best teams.

Booker scans the court as he drives toward the hoop.

Booker remains committed to winning a championship for Phoenix. In July 2022, he signed a contract extension with the team. He said, "Phoenix, thank you for allowing me to grow. The love from this city has been there from the beginning."

As a guard, a big part of Booker's job on the court is to handle the ball.

DEVIN BOOKER CAREER STATS

GAMES:
477

POINTS:
11,217

ASSISTS:
2,228

REBOUNDS:
1,865

STEALS:
398

THREE-POINTERS:
978

Stats are accurate through the 2021–2022 NBA season.

GLOSSARY

assist: a pass to a teammate that leads to a score

COVID-19: an infectious disease that emerged in late 2019 and spread around the world

draft: when teams take turns choosing new players

fadeaway: a jump shot made while jumping away from the basket

guard: a player stationed in the backcourt, away from the basket, who directs team play

recruit: an athlete who is likely to succeed at the next level

rookie: a first-year player

scholarship: money given to a student to help pay for their education

triple-double: having double-digit totals in three categories out of five (points, rebounds, assists, blocks, and steals) in a single game

varsity: a school's top-level team

SOURCE NOTES

9 Marc J Spears, "Stuntin' like His Daddy: How Devin Booker's Father Paved His Way to the NBA," Andscape, November 22, 2016, https://andscape.com/features/stuntin-like-his-daddy-devin-booker-father-paved-his-path-to-the-nba/.

13 Ben Roberts, "Shooting Guard Booker Excited to Get UK Offer," *Lexington (KY) Herald-Leader*, April 27, 2013, https://www.kentucky.com/sports/college/kentucky-sports/uk-recruiting/article44421165.html.

19 Jackson Thompson, "The Phoenix Suns' Devin Booker Said Early Career Advice from Kobe Bryant to Limit Fast Food Has Helped Him Stay Durable on the Court," Insider, April 8, 2022, https://www.insider.com/devin-booker-kobe-bryant-advice-helped-limit-fast-food-2022-4.

27 "Suns' Devin Booker Signs 4-Year Supermax Contract Extension," NBA.com, July 9, 2022, https://www.nba.com/news/devin-booker-signs-extension-with-suns.

LEARN MORE

Flynn, Brendan. *The NBA Encyclopedia for Kids*. Minneapolis: Abdo Reference, 2022.

Jr. NBA
https://jr.nba.com/

Leed, Percy. *Kobe Bryant: NBA Champion*. Minneapolis: Lerner Publications, 2021.

Phoenix Suns
https://www.nba.com/suns

Sports Illustrated Kids: Basketball
https://www.sikids.com/basketball

Whiting, Jim. *The Story of the Phoenix Suns*. Mankato, MN: Creative Education, 2023.

INDEX

Booker, Melvin, 8–10
Bryant, Kobe, 18–19

Calipari, John, 13, 16
COVID-19, 4

Final Four, 15

Moss Point High School, 10–11

NBA Draft, 16

Paul, Chris, 22

Towns, Karl-Anthony, 14

University of Kentucky, 5, 12–16

PHOTO ACKNOWLEDGMENTS

Image credits: AP Photo/Rick Scuteri, p. 4; AP Photo/Kevin C. Cox/Pool Photo, pp. 6, 7; AP Photo/Andrew A. Nelles, pp. 8, 11; Al Bello/Getty Images, p. 9; Bobby McDuffie/Icon Sportswire/Corbis/Icon Sportswire/Getty Images, p. 12; Charles Bertram/Lexington Herald-Leader/Tribune News Service/Getty Images, p. 13; Andy Lyons/Getty Images, p. 14; Nick Laham/Getty Images, p. 16; Elsa/Getty Images, p. 17; Christian Petersen/Getty Images, pp. 19, 20, 25, 26; Kevork Djansezian/Getty Images, p. 21; Ron Jenkins/Getty Images, p. 22; Chris Coduto/Getty Images, p. 23; AP Photo/Matt Slocum, p. 27. Design elements: The Hornbills Studio/Shutterstock; Tamjaii9/Shutterstock.

Front cover: AP Photo/Rick Scuteri.